Mort á Deux

Poetry by Oliver Herschel

All writing contained within is the intellectual property of Oliver Herschel, and if you have perhaps read it or heard it somewhere else, you're either following me on Tumblr or you've met me in real life. In which case, congrats! You've discovered my secret identity.

2019 © Oliver Herschel

This is dedicated
to the people
who supported me
and taught me
how to be better.

Contained within:

Prelude: The Shattered Dam Gospel

1. Proserpine – 1

2. Glass Bottles Up – 3

3. A Letter to the Baker – 5

4. 他是死 (He is dead) – 7

5. Epitaph – 9

6. Clockman Winced – 11

7. This, of Them – 13

Scene One: Bidding Moon Good Riddance

8. Dostoevsky's Horse – 15

9. medicine – 17

10. Portrait of an Old God – 19

Exposition: Little Red Orchard Man

11. Sounds Heard at Night – 22

12. North America Lightning – 25

13. Doctrine – 27

14. Something That Feels Eternal – 28

Incitement: thoughts

15. August 12th – 33

16. Body Horror – 34

17. Summer Snow – 36

18. Locksmith – 38

19. 雨 (Rain) – 39

20. August 28th – 41

Scene Two: His own blood on his hands

21. Decay, in the earth, a corpse – 43

22. Lying Nude – 45

23. The Big Bang – 46

24. Tänder – 49

25. You Made Your Bed Now Burn With It – 50

26. 神様の骸骨 (God's Skeleton) – 52

27. 王様を殺した僕 (I Killed the King) – 53

Revelation: Pomegranate Tongue

28. Ides – 57

29. Thanatium est – 59

30. A Meditation on the Musculoskeletal – 62

31. Experiments of a Humanist – 65

32. from beyond – 66

33. Anno Domini – 68

Acknowledgements

"The feeling within begins to burst through, and with a stutter in my lungs and this heaviness in my chest, I let it all pour out in rainbow colors onto the floor with whiskey-flavored tears. It leaves a sting behind my eyes and a tremor in my throat as the liquor reaches my head and gives me the strength to let go of the inhibitions and propriety that restrain me.

I can feel my chest break, my heart escape, and I watch as the colors paint the grey room that had throttled me for so long. It comes to life in shades of blue and pink and purple.

The whiskey tears bleed into the paint until the entire room smells of the tainted mixture, so I take a deep breath and hope that some of this will last."

The Shattered Dam Gospel
December 22nd, 2017

Proserpine

-

Come, healing rain

Come and drown me

The storm has settled in my throat

And a downpour is waiting

But the clouds are thick and heavy

Sitting in the sky and blotting out the sun

The earth looks as in eternal night

Linger, does this rain

When you come I'll bathe

The heat of your storm will cleanse me

The saline water will purify

The clouds will lift and sunlight will come

Flowers will rise from the ground

2 - Proserpine

Pour it down, heavy sky

Release your oppressive weight

Take with you the burden of this land

And wash it down the drain

Clean the roads and walks as you go

Lift the weight of cloud from this earth

It's spring, sweet spring

So bring your rain

And bring the renewal and rebirth

This season promises

Sweet spring, baptize me

Let the rain fall, and let it baptize me.

Glass Bottles Up

-

"I'm self-destructive,"

"But not in the worldly way.

"Cigarettes make me choke,

And I hate the way they taste

But I notice I've craved a gasp

Despite my lasting hate.

"Liquor burns my throat,

And settles in my lungs

Passing through me it screams

And I wince.

"Sex would be nice,

But I fear the embrace

Distrusting the world

4 - Glass Bottles Up

I couldn't give in."

"My destruction festers within

In my throat and lungs

But it's metaphysical

And I want it to be real."

A Letter to the Baker

-

When I was 16,

You loved me deeply

You lingered on forever

You embraced my youth

When I was 16,

My feelings were empty

Hollow and cruel and astounding

And I could not love you

Four years now, I don't talk to you

But I remember how it was

The idea of what you were

And I find your ghost alive in my chest

Four years on, my brain still wiring

6 - A Letter to the Baker

And it thinks thoughts that trace to you

You were so good, and now grown

Who are you now? I want to know

And introduce you to

Who I am now.

他是死

I hear your drums

They beat and beat and strike

Into my spine and ribs

Clenching on my throat

Gripping with the fingers of a killer

Beneath it all I can feel a thrum of life

The sickly string of ill-defined muscle

The flow of blood through thick and aching veins

My neck and my wrists and all the vertebrae

Piled up and stacked, one atop another

Climbing and climbing like Babel

Toward the sky and my tongue will slip

And my words are not mine

But belonging instead to someone else

He's a comfort in death

8 - 他是死

Smoke on his lips and ash in his lungs

His feelings expand and smother the vents

No air can get in the room, no light

Does he laugh? Does he cry?

Does he suffocate with us?

他是死和我是神

I will live as he dies

In my arms? Perhaps

My feelings expand and choke in his throat

And while I am here, he cannot be

I am dead, and he is God.

That's how it was supposed to be.

Epitaph

Time, the ocean, curls

Tides pushed forth by the moon, drawing closer and swallowing the ground

Fluid a force and pouring

Over rocks emerging from its bed, edges sharp and gasping for breath

Crushing, in moments

Grasping for purchase on the pulverized earth, with gaping maw, devouring

The old man stands on the shore

The sting of the sand and the things that live in the sand, and in the water

The oldest beings

Deep in the darkness, that which science cannot yet see, flourishing

He thinks of their bones

He thinks of his own, and they rattle and breathe inside of him, disassociated

10 - EPITAPH

The old man stands on the shore

He takes a step forward, and the ocean curls for him, like a second skin

The oldest beings

With hands, alarmingly human hands, outstretched they beckon him forward

He thinks of their bones

Their teeth, razor sharp, decorating the smile that welcomes him, deep beneath

Time, the ocean, curls

Their arms curl, and he curls too, into them and apart of them until he becomes them

Fluid a force and pouring

Out, into the waves, cascades of red and all of the pieces of him they reject

Crushing, in moments

Like these, with the water red and churning, and finally, *finally*, he lives.

Clockman Winced

-

Maybe I've been reading too much into this.
You have your own path in life, and I have mine.
I should be fine with this.

Do you remember the way your hand fit in mine?
It was larger, and warmer
But you never let go

Maybe I've been thinking too much about this.
You're far gone and haven't thought of me since.
I would have been fine with this.

I remember the type of person I was back then.
My mind was fixed on me, me, me
And how could you fit into such a narrow track?

I would have been fine with this.
Back then, I left you stranded
Stepping away from a castle – finished on your end,
but not on mine.

I remember the dreams I had of you
The way you climbed into my consciousness
He never did, but maybe I felt for you

But I'll argue, I couldn't
The train would have killed you

12 - Clockman Winced

I feel like it did
You died in my brain and chest.

I'm no longer fine with this
The time was too early for me
But the time was just right as well

If I could meet you again, I would
Know that, please, know that
I believe I've come to me well enough to meet you.

This, or Them

They submerged my tongue in Radium
to give me power.

They painted me in silver
to give me value.

They replaced my eyes with diamonds
to give them a hollow sparkle.

They replaced my blood with Mercury
to give me a place among the stars.

They put a computer in my brain
to give me logical thought.

They cuffed my wrists in gold
to give me meaning.

They made my price as high as they could
to give me over with profit.

"The first things I remember, thinking about my youth, are my mother's nails. When I was young, they were long, thick. Unsteady, even. I always thought they would break off if they did too much.

She doesn't have long nails anymore. They all broke off, got in the way, at one moment or another.

I suppose I was right, then.

There's a part of me that misses those nails, but there's a part of me that remembers them vividly. They were the kind of nails that could hurt me, have before – even if by accident. They're the kind I will remember and fear, and the kind that drives my own fingers to be carved at like a block of marble preparing for a gallery show."

Bidding Moon Good Riddance

April 16th, 2018

Dostoevsky's Horse

-

Watch me stand on the burning earth

With flames crawling on my legs

And smoke, ash settled in my lungs

I stand at the gutted rock

Where the giants pried it open

And humanity goes to shout.

Watch me stand at the bottom of the sea

The darkness becomes me, I become it

I begin to glow, to hunt with razor sharp teeth

Feet solid on overgrown steel

The light of the sun reflecting in my eyes.

Maybe I'll stand among the gods

In their conglomerate they keep me

I belong to their masses

16 - Dostoevsky's Horse

As easily as they belong to me.

Lungs filling up

The ocean grows thick

It coats the ash in my throat

With the ash of the sea.

There's a fire on the waves.

There's a fire in my brain.

Lungs filling up

The air grows thick

Freezing the blood in my throat

I dry up from the inside.

Medicine

I find myself in need

Of chemical release

A mistaken and empty perception

And cruel impasse

Hitched to the blurred, obscured

Brainless mindless pitch

Head full of words heart full of

Voices screaming out ideology

Barred head barred brain

Kept from me by insincerity

Who can I answer to

When these sounds and images

Around me within me

Keep rushing by me and past

And into the past and the future

And feed into me poetry of the deceased

18 - Medicine

Tongues denial and hearts rival

Empty headed imagery and veniality

To the bedded men women beasts

Clicking tongues whatever could be

Done to and unto and within

Cyber spiderwebs speeding out from fingers

Burdening me and my fingers at these keys

Clicking keys resonating through resonating skull

A mind entangled in string

Falling and encasing and becoming once more

Sandalwood incense rosemary mistletoe

Ivy to my throat and burned by matches

Struck at a pommel stone

Stuck up in an empty full throat.

Portrait of an Old God

-

Are you a demon or some kind of eldritch terror?

I swear I feel from you some sort of claw plunged deep into my chest

Talons scraping the edges of the casing and coming away soaking

A demon or an eldritch terror, why should I bother?

Even with a hand around my throat, I'd fall limp to your mercy

Even if I feel full and at ease in violent flesh, you press to me

Too deep into the filthy grey and dripping pink

Who are you and how have you come into my head time and time again?

What is it torturing me? You or the divine?

Or are you just the hand at my waist on moonless nights. The promising mouths and fingers that trace

Drawing, drawing like you do, making constellations in my skin

20 - Portrait of an Old God

Using the tips of your fingers, but never break skin

Your fingers are at my chest, but in my head I see knives

Your fingers are at my throat, but on my tongue I taste blood

Your weight at my back, but I hear the cracking of my own brittle bones

Are you a demon, something eldritch, something holy? Are you a design of my own mind come to haunt me?

Let go or hold tighter, but please let me live and revel in solitude in peace.

"In my head, I'm throwing apples at the wall. They hit with a dull crunch and burst open with a spray of white.

One after another, until my shoulder begins to ache and the wall begins to buckle. I want to throw more. I want to throw heavier things, but the only thing I have on hand is another apple. And another one. Limitless and all-consuming mountains of red, green, and yellow apples, all piled behind me.

One after another, I throw them into the wall until it breaks, and I can't do any more damage.

And yet it somehow feels safer to destroy each wall one by one, on the inside, rather than destroy them on the outside.

What is it that brought me here? That is something I can't help but wonder. Perhaps the sound it makes – the sound my head gives to many things, but for now this. *Do you find this cathartic?* I'll ask my mind. Of course, I get no answer. Only more apples."

Little Red Orchard Man

May 30th, 2018

Sounds Heard at Night

-

With a broiling brain

The frost creeps

Cellars and gutters alike all sing

Harmonies of damned ye have abandoned

Fate, with their strings or their scars

Marked onto the trunk of an overgrown tree

Some life is the sap that trickles down

And fills the carvings they make

With stagnant blood

Drawing flies

The soul becomes a swamp

The tongue a leech

Ice comes in thickets

Buries and kills, swims into lungs

Deep grey sings in tandem

23 - Sounds Heard at Night

With ribbons of blue and red

Symphony of bones

Violins of sinew

A bow to the strings and a long cry

A sob that rings out

To depths and the finish

The marrow of bones rotting deep inside

Harmonies of the damned

Played for audiences of the divine

The song spills from Goodman's throat

And among him are the scandalized

A cry that fetters out

Into the barrows and throats of wights

And the forsaken souls wail

And the faeries dance, their captives dance

With bleeding feet on fields of thorns

24 - Herschel

With broiling brain

And stagnant blood

The Goodman sins and sings

And the ghouls that sleep in the trees

Sing with him.

North America Lightning

-

Fire in the sky

Bring the storm inside

Liquid heat on my tongue

And raging white behind my eyes

Piercing, striking veins

The sight, the feeling these nerves make

Kintsugi in the clouds

Dipped in bleach and shouting

A god yells, a pagan god

Is he yelling for me

Fire in the sky

Fire in my throat, my veins

Snakes twine around my feet

Your eyes to burn into me

26 - North American Lightning

A pagan god yells with every strike

Closer closer I hear it

Crawling across the bends of the earth

To me at my windowsill

The fire dies inside the pagan god

Standing in my backyard he yells

To me, my soul unattached

Spiders on my skin and snakes in my veins

I call one but another calls me

White kintsugi in my backyard

With no water following, no water drowning.

Doctrine

-

Clench it with a balled-up fist

Don't dare release the grip

Choking and sputtering, seething ache

Can it be fixed by tears

Blanketed hope, and riddling words

Heat gets the head too quick

Hope, faith, temperament lost

Rolled into tears, threaten to spill

A sour mind repeats, regresses

Curled in a ball, spiritual, progresses

Hide from solitude in solitude

Look in a balled-up fist

Pandora's box opened

Everything lost.

Something That Feels Eternal

-

The liars' voices are thunderous, and they love to talk.

Their messages, straightforward, plain, and repeated—like a record, skipping backward, broken.

The liars' voices are monstrous, and they grab your ears, stick their mouths to them. Covering your ears, you want to block it out—

They're in your head.

It's the heart that tells you to take the knife, to take the gun.

The heart weeps—and before you didn't know what it means, but now you do.

You know why solitary confinement rots the mind.

29 - Something That Feels Eternal

Curled up and bleeding from the eyes—muffling your sounds, biting your tongue—

The loneliness rotted you.

You vaguely remember human touch.

You remember an arm around you, pulling you in. Heat and human presence.

But your corpse is too cold and your tongue too heavy—you cannot show gratitude.

You look for a god that loves you. You look for anyone to love you. Something/Anything to make you feel alive inside.

You do not believe in reincarnation. You do not believe in an all-defying love.

30 - Herschel

It's the heart: tells you to take the knife to the soft part of your chest. tells you to take the gun to the back of your throat.

You know it hurts. It hurts now, yesterday, tomorrow. It will, and it has. You think it owns you, and perhaps it does.

It's the flesh that yearns for human touch. That reaches out and longs for something not entirely platonic.

The mind is a foe to all things, and it is a battle you don't think you can win.

"Life is lapses.

In judgement: I start thinking about what it means to die. The scene that descends upon me is empty darkness that crawls into every crevice of my mind. Or it's a blank slate - reincarnate. Still me, but there are no memories of the life led before. I don't know that I am someone new. Another voice supposes the existence of souls.

Energy (humanity, the soul) cannot be created or destroyed.

The mind works through signals, like a current. But is it the mind or the soul?

In experience: I take a step back and consider my emotions, my thoughts, perspective of the world. Myself, versus people who are 2, 6, 10 years older than me. The way I think, versus the way they do. The crime of being juvenile. The punishment as education.

And memories race, slip around like ribbons on batons. They curl through rivulets of wind and only arrive when they're needed, but the rest of the time, it's soft.

The mind and its memories like a peach, in color and texture, continues through the passing of time.

In connection to humanity: A voice that cannot bear to speak rises in an empty room. People are beyond and without. The creature in the room is not human, but pretends to be. It carries with it worlds it has not seen, and holds out a hand to those who try to feed it.

Palm faced out. No, thank you."

thoughts

July 9th, 2018

Maybe, I'd tell him.

Maybe I've changed

I've been alone

For a long time.

August 12th

Body Horror

-

She balances a needle on the tip of her nail

Grins and grins with teeth like an eel

An eider slips from beneath the box-spring

Leeches borne forth from the vents

The paint chips, and wallpaper peels

And her smile beams though her teeth spill

From her mouth and to the floor, overflow

Like avalanches vomited from her mouth

Her clothes are soaked in the oil that drips

Tears falling from the gaps in the ceiling

She does not notice – I assume as she stands

35 - Body Horror

Still, oh so still, perfectly still

The needle falls, and her eyes roll out

Her heart bursts forth from her chest

Her nails, long and sharp, curl down to the root

And her mouth opens wide, as if to shout

Nothing comes forth, an omen of death

The wood below us rots away.

Summer Snow

—

I believe in the power of words

Their bludgeoning weight

And the things I fear to say

Are the things I fear to name

I feared naming the cold

Seeping into my soul

Killing the bounties of fruit

I had tended since birth;

Silently, I named it winter

And avoided seeing its face

A horrid ugly thing I feared

But felt its stinging hate

I feared naming the plague

That settled over the land

Held limply in my hands

37 - Summer Snow

My plenty I could not keep;

In my head were only images

Of the crops turning to ice

The food I'd cultivated

Growing brown as they thirsted

The power of word filled me

Poems dedicated to my dying fields

But unnamed was the source

Until it forced my gaze;

The monster was cold

Its eyes were sharp

As the ice that covered it

It named itself, wordlessly

For a moment, we shared a mind

And I spoke the word aloud

Knowledge rushed past like wind

Meeting its gaze, I felt nothing.

Locksmith

-

You speak freely with your lips

What is that? How is that?

Where does the key lie?

When I was a child, I locked them

And now everything boils inside.

You speak freely with your hands

With your tongue and with your teeth

You allow your mind to race and rant

And the words spill, flood the room

You speak, and we drown as rats.

You know what you think

I know what I think, too

So the only difference remaining

Is the fact that you speak

While I build a silent room.

雨

-

The smoke in our lungs is made of us

And we breathe in with deep breaths our elders

Tall as they are, broad and brooding

Speckled in the distance, lining the skyline

Giants exhaling our life, immovable ancestors

Against our own, in their arms, I feel safe

Flesh of my flesh and blood the same

I dance with you when the feeling arises

Us, dressed in green, red, and brown

Kin to you and you to me

Press myself into your presence

To the skies we rise and drift

Hephaestus devours us and the weak perish

Our choirs fall, but no sound comes from us

40 - 雨

We are the only ones who can hear

Soundless screaming, built

Only now in the present

Bare – our costumes burnt away

Faces raised to an unforgiving sun

I speak with words, human sounds

In every language I know, invoking our need

Looking for whichever god will respond.

A question sat on my lips

Unknown to me

It sat and burrowed into my skin

Blossoming red flesh scarred by curiosity

Answers rested on the tips of my fingers

Frozen stiff by the winter breeze

I tore the question away from me

And swallowed it down into my lungs

It expanded within me

Until I could not breathe

The question sat heavy in my chest

And I had no choice but to choke on it.

August 28th

"It's like a cavity brushing up against something sweet. A heated twinge in the chest. Like the ribcage is all rotted over and covered in waste. It feels as though I've done something wrong, but I can't place the feeling.

I've got both hands around something, but I can't tell what it is. Maybe it's a neck, maybe it's my own neck. Would I feel guilty for holding on and never letting go, or would it feel worse to keep it captive?

There's a feeling of guilt settling in my chest, but I can't figure out the reason for it. Is it my soul? Does it feel as though its persistence is a sin?

It's strange. When you first commit a sin, you feel guilt. When you continue with it, you stop feeling as though what you're doing is wrong.

If living is a sin, then I've gotten to the point where it doesn't feel wrong."

His own blood on his hands

August 29th, 2018

Decay, in the Earth, a Corpse

-

Mouth is filled with dirt

Stomach filled with dirt

Upper and lower intestines too

It's all coated, and threatens

The particles, the pieces

Coating and becoming mud

Sliding into crevices that never existed

Mouth is filled with dirt

Acid in the stomach bubbles

Broils, fills up, slips up

The esophagus burns

Wash from the inside

Purify from the inside

Cast away mud with burning lake

44 - Decay, in the Earth, a Corpse

Mouth is filled with dirt

Ears are full, eyes are full

Nose is full, I breathe it

Buried beneath layers

Living within it

Move with dirt and keep it

Lungs are full of dirt

Brain is full of dirt

My coffin had no lid

The worms made me their home.

Lying Nude

-

I am untainted.

Not caressed by gentle wind, but stale indoor air

Comfort of living, this music drowning my ears

Obscured by feather-down blankets

My body curls, sprawls, breathes in

Pillow supports me, holds my head up

Lying, taking in the feeling of existing

Existing a meaning that was always mine

This time held inside me with its head on me

Existing outside of reality and swimming.

The Big Bang

-

Helplessly, the wind stops

And the ground beneath my feet grows warmer

It is my whisper

That bangs through the quiet nights

It is my call

That rises in the forest

When the forest is empty

If I die

And lay my body down

Swallowed up by the earth

If I boil

And that which rises from me

Becomes me

And I become a new entity

Will my word be written and believed

47 - The Big Bang

Will the sanctity I preach

Infect ears for millions of years

If I die

And my body is burned

And sent off to sea

And the sea around me churns

If my body is burned

And burns the sea around me

Until both it and I are swallowed heartlessly

By plastic and refuse

If I whisper

And my gospel reaches the trees

Caresses them

Sets them ablaze

Helplessly, the wind blows

And into the air, I raise my hands

48 - Herschel

With the power of my spirit

I encase the world

Until it is I that takes the beating

Gaia's tongue between my lips

Her words in my voice

My voice in her

Intertwined, entangled into androgyny

Helplessly, the sea churns

Hands inside the ocean reach up

The entities, the ghosts inside, are angry

The individual gods of billions of lives

Neptune on their lips, scream

A siren song, a mandrake's cry

Altogether, the world as one

Bursts

Tänder

these poisoned teeth
promised something
unattainable but still
just there, out ahead
venomous fingertips
reach out to grab it
stain it, and dye gray
decades of effort; is
now flushed down a
drain. the teeth are
clenched. forward
comes an unending
defeat.

You Made Your Bed
Now Burn With It

-

I've broken my own damn heart again.

Because I have problems

Talking about what's on my mind

To the people who care for me

Because the people who care for me

Have given me reason to have problems

Talking about what's on my mind.

So I stab myself in my own chest

And I tell myself to talk to someone

About the bleeding mess my shirt is becoming

But the bleeding mess my shirt is becoming

Because I stabbed myself in my own chest

Is not what I talk to that someone about.

51 - You've Made Your Bed...

I'll lay on the floor in a pool of my own blood

And talk to myself about what's on my mind

But it's hard to solve a problem that way

It's hard to solve a problem alone

When you're lying in a pool of your own blood

Talking to yourself about what's on your mind.

The problem is with the person who cares

And it's getting harder to talk to them

Because you avoid the problem

But when you avoid the problem

It gets harder to talk to them

And the problem will always be with

The person who cares

Broke my damn heart again.

神様の骸骨

-

I've got a god

With skeletal hands

That rest on my shoulders

Face obscured by tattered fabric

I don't look back to see it

Do these eyes glow?

This god of mine

In crows and ravens

Open beaks and open claws

God is awake in their every cry

And when they hop ever so

Closer to me, they come

I feel it again

The love of my god.

王様を殺した僕

-

What is the difference

between the mask and the man?

    If the man wears the mask

        for too long, does he become it?

What is the difference

between the figment and reality?

    What form of reality

    are we in right now?

I can sing my songs to me

I can sing my songs to me

But it doesn't negate the fact I'm me

It doesn't make me not me

I can sing my songs to me

I can sing my songs to me

But it can't make me not me

54 - 王様を殺した僕

Who is the man? Who is the man?

    If I cut all my hair off

    would that make me the man?

Who is the mask? Is the mask the man?

    Why do I feel so angry?

    Why do I feel so upset?

    Why do I feel like the mask

    has been glued to my skin?

I can sing my songs to me

I can sing my songs to me

But that won't make them not by me

It won't change that I wrote them

I can sing my songs to me

I can sing my songs to me

But that won't make me like them

It won't make me like this skin

55 - Herschel

This skin! I've been tethered to

> Why do I feel like the mask
>
> has been glued to my skin?

This skin I've been fastened to

> Why do I feel like my body
>
> was stitched to my soul
>
> forcefully?

This skin I've been stuck to

> I'll tear at you
>
> I'll tear at you
>
> I'll tear you away from me

Why do I feel like the mask has been glued to my skin?

I can sing my songs to me

I can sing my songs to me

But I can't make the horse drink

I can't make the horse drink.

"She stays with him. She is with him even now. The proof of it rests on my skin and tickles my nose.

Some people say that Persephone was kidnapped. Some people say that the marriage had been brought on by abduction, that she was unhappily wed, that she was forced into the situation.

As I get colder, and colder, and colder, and as the nights go longer, and longer, and longer: I have trouble believing that is so. I bury myself in snow, I entomb myself in ice and crystalline flakes that preserve their shapes when they land on my scarf.

Let me have this one thing, I want to plead. Let me see at least one of them happy.

Let me desire something from these gods. What lies between Persephone and Hades: that is all I have.

It stays colder the longer she stays, but as I lie alone at night under heavy blankets, imagining my skeletal god descending on me, I do not blame her."

Pomegranate Tongue

[February 16th, 2019]

Ides

I've been looking at my reflection

Brother, I can't see your face

I've been looking in the mirror

Brother, I can't picture my face

I used to see the future, brother

I used to see where my life would lead

Imagine a time beyond all this, brother

I used to picture how I would live

But I can't see it anymore

Brother, I've been here before

I know where this empty goes

Brother, I'm afraid of this road

Hell waits at the end, brother

58 - Ides

My throat will start to scream for rope

Death waits at the end, brother

The knife, the gun, god, I'm scared

Brother, show me your face

Please I need something to hold onto

Brother, show me my face

Please I need to know something's in the future.

Thanatium est

I.

He drinks now of the water vitae

The strong, brave one; unfallen

He drinks and with his gaze, sees

Skies that reach down; beckon

With burdening blanket of gray

The waters lead him to Hades

The Underworld, ancients say

Where the old dead find haven

He walks the shores of Lethe

Retreating from the old omen

He bathes in the cursed waterway

And he is fed as another casualty

II.

Of myself, he who seeks Death

That which is called, acts as

The faceless mask, the holy

A ghost of flesh, heir of Venus

The Roman roads; a halted breath

He who becomes consumes mythology

III.

O! Osiris drinking from whispers

Words unspoken and unheeded

The baseborn son kneels in front

If the scales tip, if his fate gaunt

Will he forgive himself his terrors

To be entombed in this ballad

IV.

The forsaken dead, among them lay

A woman of two undead faces won

61 - HERSCHEL

Restful solitude from the deceased

The forsaken dead, father of the sun

Whose drifting coffin strikes the bay

Rotting corpse but living, he breathes

$\underline{\nabla.}$

Hold aloft your drinks, brothers

And see not Heaven divided

The gods war, keep solid front

Never mind the lurking savant

Hidden in shadows, yourself blinded

And never free of Fate's actors.

A Meditation on the Musculoskeletal

-

My bones are the only things truly mine

Kneeling at the altar, my bones float

Crash into nerves that pinch me screaming

I can move I can move I embrace that

But the anguish I felt in my brain has

Migrated throughout the rest of me

They migrated throughout the rest of me

These bones, the only things truly mine

In my brain, the anguish I feel

While kneeling at this altar, bones afloat

And I move, still I move, and embrace it

Bones crashing into nerves, pinching, screaming

I'll scream, as my bones pinch these nerves

63 - Meditations on the Musculoskeletal

As they migrate throughout the rest of me

Still I'll move, I'll move, exacerbate it

Because these things are the only truly mine

Resting on them, at the skeletal god's altar

With no more anguish in my brain

Yet that anguish I had felt inside my brain

The neurons crashing, reducing me to screaming

Kneeling at my god's altar, I'll float

That anguish migrated throughout me

To the only things left that are truly mine

They make me move, move, I love them

Here I move here I move, embrace it

But the anguish I felt in my brain has

Spread to the only thing truly mine

Crash into nerves that pinch me screaming

Migrating to what's left of me

Kneeling at the altar, the anguish floats

64 - Herschel

Kneeling at the altar, the bones float

Watch them move, move and exalt them

It's migrating throughout the rest of you

That anguish you once felt in your brain

Crash into nerves and pinch you screaming

These bones remain the only things truly mine

Migrating throughout the rest of me

While I kneel at the altar, floating in air pockets

My bones are the only things truly mine

With them I move I move I embrace that

The anguish I once felt in my brain now

Crashes against nerves that pinch me screaming

Experiments of a Humanist

-

The Earth Mother carries us in her core, and in the sheen of her womb we grow, but even if we grow we emerge and become parasites that cannot remember what it is to be pre-

natal.

The oceans rise up and swallow the earth and we, like the fish we used to be, slink back into the seas into the waiting tentacles of the Gods That We Destroyed when we became bipedal, but we are no longer safe from them now we are post-

naval.

The Horsemen, innumerable, and outranking the archangels stand on an unbeaten shore of perfectly round rocks as the storm of cataclysm rages around them, and when they look toward the lightning and toward the death of the Earth Mother, they see

humanity.

from beyond

-

i do

find you

a lover sweet

好小死睡觉

i find

the words you say

sooth

folie-á-mort;

c'est moi et ce

you sing me to sleep,

and i go to sleep　　　　　　大丈夫

弟君

僕らが　　　　　　　助けて

and when

you sing to me

                              i go to sleep

    死

                                    喜欢

            我和你

                            when

               you sing to us

      we rest,   we fall to leaves

et il chante

    il chante mon petít frére endormir

Anno Domini

-

I missed the day

I missed it by twelve days

As I was running,

I fell and my bones

jumped out of me

And I needed to stop

and pick them all up

I've misplaced them

and the preacher

sitting on the wall, watching

laughed and said,

"That's God's Plan."

ACKNOWLEDGEMENTS

-

This is the part of the book where I get all sentimental, or at least it was in *Fear*, and I'm not changing that this time.

First, I want to thank the people who know me in real life, especially the ones that had to sit through me reading my poetry to them. I am sorry for putting you through that; it was embarrassing for both of us.

Second, my friends online who supported me and let me know what they thought of my writing. It's really awesome having you guys there for me.

Also, kudos to my brain for not being the thing I was writing about near the latter half of this one.

And lastly, thank you, dearest reader, for picking up this book. I hope you enjoyed it.

43659416R00052

Made in the USA
Middletown, DE
27 April 2019